The (Almost) Painless
ISO 9001:2015
Transition

The (Almost) Painless ISO 9001:2015 Transition

Denise Robitaille

Paton
PROFESSIONAL

Chico, California

Most Paton Professional books are available at quantity discounts when purchased in bulk. For more information, contact:

Paton Professional
PO Box 44
Chico, CA 95927-0044
Telephone: (530) 342-5480
Email: books@patonprofessional.com
Web: www.patonprofessional.com

20 19 18 17 16 15   10 9 8 7 6 5 4 3 2 1

ISBN: 978-1-932828-70-2

Library of Congress Cataloging in Publication Data on File

Staff
Editor & Publisher: Scott M. Paton
Assistant Editors: Daniel Taylor and Laura Smith
Book design: Anita Jovanovic
Cover design: Miguel Kilantang

Contents

Introduction

ISO 9001 has had center stage in the quality arena for more than a quarter of a century. Globally, it's the premier quality management system (QMS) model upon which many sector-specific standards are based. It has broad acceptance across an expansive and varied spectrum of users due to its nonprescriptive, generic nature and its broad applicability. This widespread appeal increases the mandate for updating ISO 9001 to ensure its continued relevance in an ever-changing world.

The ISO 9001:2015 revision process started almost five years ago. Even before the committee draft was issued, a considerable amount of work had already been expended on this latest revision. Considering the fact that the number of ISO 9001 registrations around the globe exceeds 1.2 million, the attention given to the revision wasn't unwarranted.

The transition to the new standard has generated a great deal of debate and much upheaval. Opinion, fact, misinformation, unqualified interpretations, and reliable publications all share the same stage, compounding the confusion. It's no wonder that the transition process has come to be perceived with such obvious consternation.

This book is intended to ease the transition from ISO 9001:2008 to ISO 9001:2015. It will lay out the essential differences between the two versions so that you can develop the necessary plans for your organization to move forward with your transition. This approach is consistent with one of the general requirements of the standard, as found in clause 4.1 of ISO 9001:2008 and clause 4.4 of ISO 9001:2015. These clauses direct an organization to identify its processes and determine the sequence, interaction, and criteria for operation and control. ISO 9001:2015 includes language that's relevant to this transition. It requires an organization to understand the internal and external issues that affect its ability to achieve its goals. You can use the transition process itself to begin to fulfill this requirement. Understanding these factors will help define the scope and the nature of your transition project.

Consistent with its generic nature, the standard also recognizes that issues such as the method of implementation, level of control, and mechanism for monitoring are unique to each organization. What constitutes adequate definition and control for a hardware distributor will be substantially different for a pharmaceutical manufacturer or a software developer. What makes sense for your organization may be irrelevant to another.

The good news and the bad news for this transition project are the same: The decisions are yours. You have the freedom to develop, implement, and modify your QMS so that it's meaningful and beneficial to your organization, utilizing ISO 9001 as a framework. With that freedom comes the responsibility to give proper and conscientious consideration to the manner in which your system is defined, provisioned, deployed, controlled, monitored, and improved. This responsibility lies at the foundation of section 5 in both ISO 9001:2008 and ISO 9001:2015. Top management involvement must be consistent and visible. In fact, the language in subclause 5.1.1 of ISO 9001:2015 specifically states that the organization's leadership is responsible for "…[T]aking accountability for the effectiveness of the quality management system." Consequently, it's important that the organization's leadership have input into this transition process.

To realize the optimum efficiency intended by the use of this book, it's important to understand how it's laid out. Part I discusses the implications for your QMS. It covers both new concepts and actual changes in requirements. Although some of the changes and additions target a specific element or function in your organization, others permeate your entire QMS.

Part II is organized to help you assess your system. This will in turn direct you back to explanations in earlier chapters to help you understand what you must do to implement the changes.

This book is targeted at organizations that have decided to transition to ISO 9001:2015. It's not intended—and therefore will have only limited value—for those who are new to ISO 9001. The book provides a methodological approach to determining what processes are currently compliant, which ones need work, and what processes or features have to be added. Culling the vital few will streamline the process and dispel most of the confusion.

This book may provide additional support in the transition process for those companies that have experienced lapses in the maintenance of their QMS or that have persistent problems that have eluded corrective action. It's possible that this assessment and implementation project will shed new light on processes and result in unanticipated improvements.

This is a logical process. ISO 9001:2015 introduces new concepts that facilitate development of plans for both operational activities and fulfillment of strategic goals. Given adequate attention, this transition process will be a beneficial and value-added experience. Good luck!

Chapter 1

What's Happened?

ISO 9001 has been revised. The process has taken almost five years with a lot of input from varied sources and technical experts. Throughout the process the reactions from users have ranged from mild curiosity to excitement to extreme trepidation. The latest revision to ISO 9001 has generated unprecedented interest and media frenzy in the quality community. And the hype has not been unwarranted.

It's important to bear in mind that the 2008 revision was a minor one, with no new or changed requirements. This means that the standard hadn't had a significant makeover since 2000.

THE REVISION PROCESS

The International Organization for Standardization (ISO) directives require that a standard undergo systematic review within five years of its latest release. This is similar to the requirements in any quality management system (QMS) for periodic review to ensure continued applicability and suitability. It's a good idea. Things change.

A lot has changed in our world since the turn of the millennium. Supply chains now regularly span the globe. Vast quantities of information can be transmitted virtually instantaneously. Organizations now store massive amounts of data in "the cloud." Environmental concerns are incorporated increasingly into most organizations' strategic plans. The evolution of ideas and technology has exploded—and our ability to manage it all has become increasingly critical. It is in this tumultuous environment that ISO 9001 was revised.

In keeping with its own requirements, ISO reviewed and revised ISO 9001:2008 and approved what's now known as *ISO 9001:2015 Quality management systems—Requirements*. In addition, *ISO 9000 Quality management systems—Fundamentals and vocabulary* (the normative reference for ISO 9001:2015) has also been revised.

In 2009, prior to the systematic review and anticipating a revision, members of ISO Technical Committee 176 Subcommittee Two (ISO/TC 176/SC 2), which has responsibility for the revision and maintenance of ISO 9001, began conducting an extensive user survey. It was important to solicit the kind of information the market could provide to ensure that this document remained relevant and beneficial to the users.

Feedback was sought from every industry and sector, from users of other management system standards, and even from those who have chosen not to implement an ISO 9001-compliant QMS. More than 10,000 responses were received from around the world. All these data were collated, reviewed, and analyzed.

While the survey was being conducted, a task group was established to explore concepts and ideas for a future revision of ISO 9001. Over the course of several meetings, the technical experts (as members of ISO/TC 176 are known) explored the significant global changes and evolving concepts vis-à-vis the standard to decide which ones might be relevant to any future revisions. Based on the work of the task group, several white papers were generated elaborating the justification for possible inclusion of some of the concepts.

In accordance with ISO directives, the members of ISO/TC 176 initiated a systematic review of ISO 9001 in October of 2011. The ballot choices for a systematic review are: withdraw, revise/amend, or confirm. The output of the global survey and of the task group meetings provided essential input to the participating members as they cast their votes. When the ballot closed in March 2012, the results were announced. The members of ISO/TC 176 had voted to revise/amend.

Having made the decision to revise ISO 9001, ISO/TC 176/SC 2 began laying the foundation for the work ahead. In subsequent meetings, the working group moved forward with a project plan, design specification, and working draft. Inputs into the design review process included the results of customer surveys, white papers generated from the task group on the future of ISO 9001, and ideas that had been tabled during the previous (2008) revision that had been deemed beyond the scope of a minor revision.

FOUR INFLUENCING FACTORS

There were a number of other factors that influenced the revision. Of these, there are four that warrant further discussion.

The first is the revision to the quality management principles (QMPs). This fundamental document lays the foundation for any QMS. The principles relate to the customer, leadership, people, the process approach, improvement, decision making, and managing relationships with external parties. The principles had remained unchanged for more than two decades. Although the revision to the QMPs is not dramatic, it is important. It has resulted in a slight shift of focus for organizations implementing QMSs. Two noteworthy improvements relate to the process approach and mutually beneficial supplier relations.

The revised QMPs combine "process approach" and "systems approach to management"—formerly two principles—into one. This serves to emphasize the need for organizations to recognize that effective processes are interrelated and interdependent operating in a coherent system. The final principle relating to suppliers has been renamed "Relationship Management," acknowledging the need to manage relationships, not only with suppliers but also with multiple other relevant interested parties. This is consistent with the changes introduced in section 4 of ISO 9001:2015.

More information on the QMPs is found in chapter 3.

The second factor influencing the revision was the development of a high-level structure by the Joint Technical Coordination Group (JTCG) for all ISO management system standards. The structure, along with identical core text and common terms and definitions, has been published in the ISO directives and is known as Annex SL. Its intent is to bring greater homogeneity to the systems of organizations charged with adoption of multiple management system standards. On the one hand, it has resulted in the reduction of some requirements, creating a more generic standard. On the other hand, the introduction of new concepts has generated the need for additional and, in some cases, more prescriptive requirements. These will be discussed in greater detail in subsequent chapters.

The third factor deals with the change in the users of ISO 9001. When first introduced in the mid-1980s, the standard was used primarily by the general manufacturing sector. Products were tangible. Software development was in its infancy. And service organizations represented a smaller slice of the global economic pie. As it became clear that the generic nature of ISO 9001 made it amenable to a broad spectrum of organizations, implementations soared in new fields, including software, finance, health care, and service. This merits discussion because it has resulted in some very deliberate shifts in language and in requirements. The most glaring of these is the change from "products" to "products and services" throughout the standard. It has also triggered the need for modified requirements to accommodate these new sectors. These will be discussed in subsequent chapters.

The last factor is probably the least obvious. In 2009, ISO 9004 was revised, breaking its consistent pairing with ISO 9001. Although it's no longer identified as being half of a consistent pair (with ISO 9001), it still continues to be the hallmark for improving your QMS. *ISO 9004:2009 Managing for the sustained success of an organization—A quality management approach* introduced new concepts concerning sustainable success, needs and expectations of interested parties, and the organization's environment. The kernels of these three concepts have taken root in ISO 9001:2015 in slightly modified form. They provided at least part of the impetus for the concepts found in two sections of the revised standard. Section 4 introduces the context of the organization and the requirements to understand the needs and expectations of interested parties. Section 6 contains enhanced requirements for greater integration of the QMS into the business processes, availability of resources, and ensuring that the system achieves its intended results.

It's worth noting that, in addition to the influence it has had on this revision, ISO 9004 has substantial benefits that may improve the effectiveness of your QMS and facilitate the transition process. ISO 9004 is a guidance document. It contains a lot of good information that can be used to enhance an existing QMS. It's a great asset. Within the text are found nuggets relating to—among other things—strategy, involvement of people, relationships with suppliers and partners, managing resources, knowledge management, and a self-assessment tool. It also contains examples of initiatives that an organization might use to grow beyond ISO 9001 by enhancing those features that would provide value for the organization and support the commitment to increase customer satisfaction. Any organization going through the transition process may wish to consider the guidance found in ISO 9004.

TRANSITION CERTIFICATION

The International Accreditation Forum (IAF), the worldwide association of conformity assessment bodies, has determined the time frame and general rules for the transition process. Registrars will cease to support ISO 9001:2008 in September 2018. If you're going to continue to have an ISO 9001-registered QMS, you have to transition to the new standard prior to that date. Basically, the transition period is three years. The certification audit for transition to the 2015 version of the standard can occur during a surveillance audit, a recertification audit, or a special visit. It's best to communicate with your registrar on the scheduling of the transition assessment. The IAF has developed a free transition guidance document that is available from its website (*www.iaf.nu*).

BENEFITS OF ISO 9001:2015 AND THE TRANSITION PROCESS

Transition for its own sake—or to maintain certification—is a paltry justification for embarking on a project to change one's QMS. It's undeniable that, for many organizations, customer demands or tacit expectations leave little latitude in the decision to transition to the 2015 version of the standard. That having been said, it's beneficial to approach this transition process with a commitment to use it to improve the organization. Stagnant practices can get an invigorating boost; new concepts can spur innovative ideas. Lackadaisical lethargy can be replaced by positive engagement as the whole QMS gets a fresh coat of paint. This can only happen if the organization makes a concerted decision to get value out of the transition. There are some great new ideas in ISO 9001:2015. Seizing the momentum from implementing them can be transformational and empowering.

The significant changes and new concepts that have been introduced will be discussed in chapter 2. All other changes will be dealt with in chapter 4, where the entire standard will be reviewed clause by clause.

WHAT MUST BE DONE

It's quite possible that new or revised ISO 9001:2015 requirements have already been incorporated into the fabric of your QMS. Some requirements make such simple business sense that companies have implemented them as a matter of course over the years. Other requirements, such as enhanced attention to interested parties or change control, might have been driven by sector-specific requirements or customer needs. If that's not the case for your organization, these additions to your QMS can be implemented with ease, building on existing processes like management review and data analysis.

There isn't one cookie-cutter approach to what must be done. The transition will vary for every organization precisely because this new version endorses using a system that best fits your organization's structure and needs.

Here are some general guidelines you can follow:
- Buy copies of both ISO 9001:2015 and ISO 9000:2015—*and read them*!
- Conduct a gap analysis to identify:*
  - ✓ What needs to change
  - ✓ What needs to be added

    *If possible, get a couple of your internal auditors to read the new standard and participate in the gap analysis.

- Create a plan for the transition process:
  - ✓ Review the results of your gap analysis to identify tasks.
  - ✓ Put together a team so they can be engaged from the onset.
  - ✓ Ensure top management involvement for two reasons:
    - Some of the most important changes affect them.
    - There will be a need for resources: time and training.

  - ✓ Establish a deadline for completion.

  Additional considerations when creating your plan:
- Conduct a management review after the gap analysis. Top management must remain informed of both the requirements and the progress toward the project goals. Also, there may be some factors outside of the scope of the transition that come to light that will also warrant management's attention and input.
- Schedule training sessions for affected departments and individuals.
- Communicate the high points of the transition plan to the entire organization through a town hall meeting or whatever method you generally employ for companywide notifications of importance.
- If the gap analysis reveals that the project will be large and elaborate, break it up into manageable chunks and assign responsibility and authority to other personnel.
- Ensure that your internal auditors get adequate and effective training.
- Determine what processes are currently compliant and which need some work. Culling the vital few will streamline the process and dispel most of the confusion. The worksheets in part II of this book will help you to control this sorting process.

- Make use of the existing good practices you have in place for controlling document revisions and training on new procedures.
- Try not to protract the transition process. You will diffuse the focus and end up wasting time. Implement the changes that you must make incrementally. Don't wait to approve all the changes at once.
- Don't consume valuable time renumbering documents. ISO 9001:2015 has language specifically noting that there is no requirement for an organization's documentation to mirror the structure of the standard. (If, however, you have compelling reasons to maintain clause number consistency, you may do so.)
- Communicate with your registrar about the transition schedule.

Above all, remember that this is your system. It must work for you.

Chapter 2

What Changed?
(Not As Much As You Think)

Relax. There is more that has remained the same within ISO 9001 than has changed. Many requirements have simply been moved around and reformatted. A fair chunk of the transition process is actually devoted to fitting the requirements into the new high-level structure of Annex SL. There are additional requirements. In most cases they should provide benefit and help the organization to fulfill its mission. The approach is still logical, with an even greater focus on integrating the quality management system (QMS) into the business processes.

Back in 2000, the standard was reformatted to disperse the "20 elements" over five sections. The process approach was introduced, and the concept of a system with interrelated processes became the model for the QMS.

The 2015 revision reinforces the process approach and introduces the concept of "context of the organization," which will be discussed in greater detail later in this chapter. The section and clause numbers have once again been changed, but the basic requirements remain relatively unchanged.

ISO 9001:2015 still has the same logical progression through an iterative cycle based on the iconic plan-do-check-act (PDCA) model originally introduced by Walter Shewhart in the first quarter of the 20th century and popularized by W. Edwards Deming after World War II. You set up a system, plan, and provide resources (**P**lan); perform all the activities that allow you to bring product to market (e.g., get customer specifications, design, purchase raw materials, produce product, inspect, identify, store, and ship) (**D**o); monitor performance, get feedback from the customer, and review the results to see what worked (**C**heck); and decide what must be improved and act on your decision (**A**ct). The cycle is continual. There can also be smaller cycles inside of larger ones.

The requirements that were formerly organized into clauses such as "contract review" or "purchasing" are still applicable. The names have changed but the requirements are either unchanged or comparable. "Contract review" morphed into "customer-related processes" with the revision from 1994 to 2000. But some organizations never changed the name of their documents. In ISO 9001:2015, "suppliers" are now referred to as "providers." However, the definition in ISO 9000:2015 notes that "supplier" is still an accepted term. "Purchasing" now comes under the heading of "Control of externally provided processes, products and services" and includes control of outsourced processes as well as consideration of products and services provided by a separate unit (e.g., a sister division) of the same organization.

Don't get overwhelmed or bogged down in the minutiae. Although some things have changed, much of your ISO 9001:2008-compliant system is fine just the way it is. You're still required to define those activities that are needed to fulfill requirements, implement them under appropriately controlled conditions, and provide records as evidence of fulfillment. As long as you're in compliance with your own procedures and with ISO 9001:2015, you can leave those processes alone and focus on what really must be addressed.

You don't need to renumber your documentation to reflect the revised standard's numbering scheme. In fact, there is no requirement to do so. The numbers have value only as quick references for looking up the applicable clauses and subclauses in ISO 9001:2015. Renumbering procedures is a time-consuming activity with little return. It does make it easier for the registrar's assessor to determine your conformance to the standard. But, a good auditor should be able to figure things out. You aren't required to accommodate the registrar's whims; you're only required to do that which is mandated by ISO 9001:2015.

DELETED AND DIMINISHED REQUIREMENTS

There are several noteworthy changes that have resulted in either deleted or diminished requirements. There are other smaller changes in language that have resulted in less prescriptive requirements. The significance of those changes will vary from one organization to the next. However, the following four changes merit discussion.

Quality manual

ISO 9001:2015 no longer requires a quality manual. However, it's important to note that ISO 9001:2015 doesn't prohibit the use of a quality manual. It's merely silent on the subject.

Prior revisions of ISO 9001 had clear and prescriptive requirements on what needed to be included in the quality manual. With the removal of the requirement, organizations now have the freedom to revise their quality manual so that it has greater value and is more reflective of the organization's character and scope. Or, they may choose to forego a quality manual altogether.

Each organization has the opportunity to assess the quality manual's value. There are multiple factors to consider:

- If an organization has multiple management system standards, it may find that one of the others, such as ISO 13485 still requires a quality manual. Similarly, there are regulatory requirements for a quality manual, such as those found in the Food and Drug Administration's 21 CFR 820—Quality System Regulation. It's also possible that customers require the organization to have a quality manual. Any of these scenarios make discussion about deleting the quality manual moot.

- Some quality manuals are terrible. They are either a fill-in-the-blanks document that regurgitates the standard or a generic off-the-shelf template with no relevance to the organization's structure, scope, market, or culture. They've been around for years—legacy documents that individuals have been loath to tamper with due to ISO 9001's requirements. Now's your chance to either pitch them or make them into something useful.

- ISO 9001:2015 continues to require organizations to define their scope and the interrelation of processes. If you make the decision to dump the quality manual (which was the traditional repository for this information), where then will the organization document these requirements?

Requirements for a quality manual may have gone away, but the decision to trash what is supposed to be a top-level document should be made with careful deliberation.

Documented procedures

ISO 9001:2015 no longer has any specific requirements for documented procedures. As a matter of fact, the word "procedure" only appears in the foreword and the annexes of the standard. It's conspicuously absent from the requirements.

Like the quality manual, it's best to simply say that ISO 9001:2015 is silent on the subject. If you have procedures and they work for you, there's no need to change the manner in which you document your internal requirements.

There is still a need to maintain documents that are deemed necessary by the organization to fulfill its mission. This is all covered under the new concept of "documented information," which is discussed later in this chapter.

This change grants organizations greater flexibility in determining how processes will be documented and controlled. In part II of this book, the individual work sheets allow you to note how activities are documented—in a procedure, work instruction, or some other method or medium. Again, more on this later.

Preventive action

The term "preventive action" has been deleted from ISO 9001:2015. It's been replaced by the concept of "risk-based thinking," which will be discussed later. This is a great enhancement. Preventive action is a good and necessary idea, and was always intended to encompass the concept of risk. Unfortunately, ISO 9001 has never provided adequate guidance or specificity. Consequently, the output of attempting to fulfill this requirement resulted in confusion, resentment, and needless paperwork. The term and the requirement for a documented procedure are gone. In contrast, risk-based thinking makes a meaningful addition to an organization's system.

Management representative

ISO 9001:2015 no longer has a requirement for an individual from management to be appointed as the management representative. Unlike the quality manual, however, the requirement has been transformed. Clause 5.3 now requires that "…Top management shall assign the responsibility and authority for…" The text that follows includes most of the language formerly found in ISO 9001:2008 under the heading of "Management Representative" and actually expands the role. So, the responsibility is diffused and may be assigned but remains within the purview of management.

Infrastructure

This is a somewhat different change. ISO 9001:2015 still requires the appropriate maintenance of the infrastructure needed to carry out processes. The requirement has been diminished in that all subsequent text relating to equipment, buildings, vehicles, etc. has been moved into a note. Notes are used for guidance and do not constitute requirements. This is one of the examples of changes that were made to be more generic and reflective of nonmanufacturing organizations. Because the language is no longer prescriptive, it creates the mandate for each organization to figure out which aspects of its infrastructure need to be maintained and controlled.

Allowable exclusions

There is no longer a requirement to cite allowable exclusions. In the past, items such as design could be excluded if the organization produced product based upon the customers' designs or specifications. Other common examples included calibration of equipment, control of customer property, and purchasing.

ISO 9001:2015 now addresses applicability. It states that the organization must provide justification for not applying any requirements of the standard. The rule is simply that if it can be applied, it must be applied. Therefore, an organization may not exclude from its QMS any requirement that can be applied to the scope of its QMS. You can't exclude processes because you want to. Any process that affects the organization's ability to provide conforming product or enhance customer satisfaction is considered applicable.

Unlike in ISO 9001:2008, exclusions (or lack of applicability) may be cited for any clause of the standard. Formerly exclusions were limited to section 7.

As a side note, there's still the need to provide justification. This was previously documented in the quality manual. If the decision is made to abandon the quality manual, the organization must decide where this justification will reside.

NEW REQUIREMENTS

Context of the organization

This requires organizations to identify the internal and external issues that affect them. It also requires them to understand the needs and expectations of relevant interested parties. It's a bit misleading to think of this as a new concept.

The language and the need to fulfill requirements in relation to these factors may be new, but the underlying principles have already been implemented to varying degrees in most organizations. Many organizations have at least a working, albeit informal, familiarity with the issues that affect them: capacity, material shortages, personnel turnover, machine breakdowns, changes in the financial markets, etc. But they may not have a systematic method for regularly monitoring these factors. ISO 9001:2015 now requires organizations to bring some consistency to their deliberations around these issues. It directs organizations to determine what issues are relevant to their purpose and, through guidance notes, gives examples of some of the tools and practices that may facilitate this process. So, the standard drives organizations to do a better job of thinking of all the issues that can affect their ability to serve their customers and to consider the risks and opportunities that are associated with these factors. Bringing consistency to what, in the past, have probably been haphazardly applied and poorly documented practices is the big benefit from this requirement.

Internal issues might include:
- Expected retirement of key personnel with specific knowledge and skills
- Addition of a second shift to accommodate increased sales
- Aging machinery or obsolete equipment
- Formation of a labor union
- Relocation of the company
- Improvement to processes
- Expiration of a government-funded training grant

External issues might relate to:
- Loss of a key supplier
- Changes in environmental regulations
- Ventures into new markets with stricter statutory constraints
- Tightening of lending guidelines from financial institutions
- Scarcity of raw materials
- Natural disasters
- Major road construction in areas that the organization services

This isn't to suggest that either of these lists are exhaustive. They merely provide a broad range of examples to demonstrate how varied and extensive the issues may be.

The other requirement relating to the context of the organization deals with understanding the needs and expectations of relevant interested parties. ISO 9000:2015 defines an interested party as a "…[P]erson or organization that can affect, be affected by, or perceive itself to be affected by a decision or activity." They are sometimes referred to as stakeholders. They may be internal (e.g., employees or owners) or external (e.g., customers, suppliers, bankers, regulators, partners, or society).

It's important to pay attention to the language of this subclause. The key word is "understand." There is no requirement to fulfill their needs and expectations. This would be impractical or impossible. Such a requirement would also exceed the scope of ISO 9001:2015, which is focused specifically on fulfilling customer requirements and enhancing their satisfaction. The point remains that, in order to serve their customers, organizations must have an understanding of how these stakeholders affect their ability to meet their organizational objectives—specifically as they relate to customers.

The last piece to this requirement is the need to monitor and review information about the internal and external issues and the relevant interested parties. Things change. What may have seemed stable and reliable could over time erode into a potential threat. Alternately, new opportunities emerge almost every day. Requirements for monitoring in this clause are aligned with another new requirement relating to change.

Planning of changes

Planning of changes is, again, not an entirely new concept. The 2008 version of ISO 9001 mentions the need to maintain the integrity of the system when changes are planned. ISO 9001:2015 adds the prescriptive text relative to planning and controlling the changes.

Change in and of itself isn't positive or negative. What makes it either a risk or an opportunity is the effect it has on planned results or intended outputs. The degree to which the output of the change can be planned, with appropriate consideration of internal and external issues, will determine whether the change results in an unforeseen problem or in an actualized opportunity. The standard clearly directs the organization to consider the purpose of the change, the potential consequences, availability of resources, and the authority and responsibility for the change. Although there is one clause relating specifically to planning changes to the QMS, the concept of change isn't relegated to that single clause of the standard—it permeates multiple sections.

Risk

As discussed earlier, the term "preventive action" no longer appears in the standard. It's been incorporated into the much more holistic concept of risk-based thinking. Preventive action deals with the potentiality of something going wrong—which is actually the essence of risk. Unfortunately, in many organizations, preventive action had been perceived as an irrelevant and disjointed nuisance with minimal significance. The manner in which the concept of risk is treated in ISO 9001:2015 makes it easier for organizations to address potential problems and take necessary action at appropriate junctures.

This creates the opportunity to foster a culture in which thinking about the consequences of change permeates all aspects of the QMS. Everyone is affected by some kind of change and, conversely, has the opportunity to have an effect on what is changing. Changes can result from the addition of a product line, the departure of key personnel, the loss of a major supplier, breakdown of a piece of equipment, a revised regulatory requirement, an increase in sales, or a whole myriad of other events. They can be small—like the revision to a document or replacement of a tool. Or they can be massive, like the relocation of the company to a new facility a thousand miles away.

Regardless of the nature or the scope, a predictable set of actions should ensue: an inquiry into the nature of the change, assessment of the risk, and a decision on what action, if any, to take.

The other enhancement to the concept of risk is the variety of choices. Formerly, with preventive action, the requirement was to take action to address causes to prevent an undesirable event or output. Language in ISO 9001:2015 accommodates the flexibility to consider the issues and make decisions that may limit the number of occurrences, mitigate the severity of the negative outcome, or result in the sharing of the risk. It also allows for the decision to take no action.

These three concepts taken uniquely have potential benefits. When you adopt the concepts of risk-based thinking, understanding the context of the organization, and change control, their interrelation and application create a synergy that cannot help but propel an organization to higher levels of effectiveness and efficiency.

Quality objectives

Quality objectives are certainly not new. What ISO 9001:2015 brings is long-overdue guidance on the need to take action to achieve the objectives. Specifically, it requires the organization to determine what needs to be done, resources, responsibility, completion time, and method of evaluating results.

This has the very positive effect of moving quality objectives from stagnant pronouncements to actionable goals: "This is our current status. That's where we want to be. This is what we will do to get there." It moves the objectives from vague potentiality to achievable possibility.

CHANGED AND ENHANCED REQUIREMENTS

Documented information

The unique concepts of documents and records have been replaced by the all-encompassing term "documented information." ISO 9000:2015 defines it as: "…[I]nformation required to be controlled and maintained by an organization and the medium on which it is contained." The salient word here is "information."

For many organizations, the information they need is no longer found in binders and paper files. Much of it is electronic or embedded in software programs such as enterprise resource planning (ERP) platforms, computer-aided design packages (CAD), manufacturing programs, or e-commerce portals—just to name a few.

Having recognized the fact that information, including requirements and specifications, is now regularly found in different and varied media, it makes sense that the language relating to the requirements is much more reflective of that diversity. It's also reflective of the increase in the multiplicity of users across a broad spectrum of industries and fields.

This shift away from the traditional procedure format is also a welcome concession to the fact that many organizations control their processes very well without the use of verbose documents that are read only by the authors, authorizers, and auditors.

Some processes are so basic that a written instruction is unwarranted and wasteful. Simple common sense should prevail. Consideration also needs to be given to the education level of workers and the ever-increasing reality of a multilingual workforce. And some processes and procedures are better understood in a picture format, regardless of the number of university degrees you have hanging on the wall. Control of a manufacturing process may be achieved by the use of any of the following methods:

- Illustrations
- Color coding

- Samples
- Jigs
- Prompts embedded in software
- Flowcharts
- Bulleted lists
- Process monitoring
- Posters
- Verbal reminders/morning meetings
- Training guides
- Many others

There have also been technological advances that have increased availability and affordability of other methods and media. For example, as recently as ten years ago, digital photography was expensive and the files used up enormous space on limited servers. Now, server capacity has increased and digital photos require just a click of the smartphone. This has enhanced the ability to cheaply embed images into electronic documents as work instructions or to use them to provide evidence of conformance.

ERP systems have eliminated the need to print purchase orders. Information is generated electronically—sometimes using automatic fulfillment parameters that preclude the need for a purchaser to even communicate with the supplier. As material is received, the purchase order moves seamlessly from the statement of requirements for purchased product to the record of receipt. The lines of the strict document/record paradigm have been blurred.

This doesn't mean that you can get rid of all the other documents. But the shift does acknowledge that the methods you use to define and control your processes are unique to your organization—which is as it should be. It would be inappropriate and foolish to attempt to impose one set of uniform rules encompassing every industry and market sector around the globe. The variables that affect definition and control are myriad and include such things as:

- Nature of the product
- Customer base
- Availability of alternate media
- Complexity of processes
- Regulatory and statutory requirements
- Environmental constraints
- Size of the organization
- Internal culture
- Number of processes
- Industry standards

Although some processes are uncomplicated, there are some at the other end of the spectrum that are complex and technically oriented. This documentation should be extremely well-developed and controlled. But even at this level, the need for a traditional procedure is not absolute. Chemists, software engineers, and toolmakers all have their own methods, protocols, and industry standards that provide guidance and impose the requisite control. Generating procedures that reiterate the same requirements is a pointless exercise.

The simple litmus test for any process should be this: In the absence of a procedure, is there adequate information and control to ensure that the process:

- Is understood by the process owner and/or operator?
- Is uniformly carried out?
- Consistently fulfills the requirements of the task?

- Has negligible risk of nonconformance or unacceptable variance?
- Can be verified?

All of this doesn't mean that you should dismantle your documentation system or throw away your procedures. You may (and probably will) discover as you go through your transition process that the most efficient way to define and control your processes is with the procedures you currently have. That's great—one less thing on the to-do list for your ISO 9001 transition project.

Another issue to consider is the increase in the number of documents and records that are accessed from remote locations that are external to the organization. For requirements, there are customers who provide their suppliers with access to a secure portal on their server where specifications, quality requirements, and drawings can be downloaded. Some even have an online corrective action module that suppliers fill out as they conduct their root cause analysis and develop their plan. The customers can monitor progress of the corrective actions and offer comments as the process unfolds. Mil Specs and regulatory requirements that formerly consumed shelves in the engineering library can now be accessed and downloaded from the internet.

Records providing evidence can also be accessed from supplier portals. Certificates of analysis, calibration certificates, and test results are routinely retained on organizations' websites to be accessed and downloaded as needed.

And, many companies are now making use of "the cloud" for storage and retrieval of their documented information. In some cases, this facilitates projects being worked on by international teams whose collaboration is largely virtual.

ISO 9001:2015 includes a note in the subclause on documented information. It emphasizes the need to differentiate between access and permission or authority. This highlights the need to ensure appropriate control of the tools that we use to manage our documented information.

One final point that will facilitate the migration to this new concept. ISO 9001:2015 hasn't totally abandoned the fundamental intent of differentiating documents from records. A quick tip as you read through ISO 9001:2015: For requirements (formerly document), the standard uses the word "maintain"; for evidence (formerly record), the word that is used is "retain." You *maintain* information relating to requirements and *retain* information that provides evidence of verifications and task completions.

The good news overall is greater flexibility that more closely mirrors the evolving methods we use to maintain, retain, and communicate information.

Management review

There are some subtle but significant changes in the requirements for management review. The first is that the standard now specifically says that management review shall be planned. The level of planning is not prescribed. However, it's valuable to consider the enhanced requirements that have been added to other parts of the standard relating to such things as monitoring internal and external issues, more prescriptive requirements around quality objectives, and the planning and control of changes. In view of these factors, it makes sense to ensure that the review process used to ensure reliable decision making and allocation of resources is well planned.

The list of items to be reviewed has been rearranged and is better organized to allow for clearer perception of interrelations and interdependencies. Processes that had their own unique classification on the list are now grouped under the general heading of trends. There have also been additions. Briefly, the list of trends now includes, among other things, customer satisfaction, feedback from relevant interested parties, process performance, conformity of products and services, nonconformities, corrective actions, audit results, and supplier performance. There's also a need to review the extent to which quality objectives have been met.

Apart from the list of trends, there are additional requirements relating to changes in internal and external issues, adequacy of resources, and effectiveness of actions to address risk.

The final interesting change is in the relocation of the requirements for management review to the clause on performance evaluation. Formerly, the gathering and analyzing of data was found in section 8, whereas the requirements for management review were found in section 5. The rearrangement of the requirements makes for a much more logical flow and creates the path from deciding what are relevant performance indicators, to the monitoring of process, to the gathering of data and analysis, to the determination of further actions to be taken.

There are multiple other changes of lesser significance. Some clarify existing requirements. Others accommodate nonmanufacturing environments. Still others improve the relevance of the standard and the benefits that can be derived.

These changes will be discussed in chapter 4.

Chapter 3

ISO 9000:2015—Why It Matters

ISO 9000:2015 presents the fundamentals and vocabulary for a quality management system (QMS). It describes the elements of a QMS, their functions, and their benefits. In contrast to ISO 9001:2015, it explains the rationale for the QMS. It provides the foundation that underlies a robust QMS. Whereas ISO 9001:2015 puts forth requirements, ISO 9000:2015 offers explanation. It provides a holistic presentation of the nature and character of a QMS.

Such concepts as the basic definition of quality, the context of the organization, and the relevance of interested parties are explained in relation to one another and as they relate to the fulfillment of organizational objectives.

ISO 9000:2015 describes a QMS not only for the benefit of those implementing ISO 9001:2015, but it also provides information about the expectations customers may have of their suppliers' QMS. Essentially, if an organization has a system that manifests the fundamentals and principles put forth in ISO 9000:2015, the customer should have confidence in the integrity of the organization's QMS.

ISO 9000:2015 developed in parallel with ISO 9001:2015. Both were revised and released during the same time period. There was extensive collaboration and interaction between the two working groups to ensure essential alignment between the requirements of ISO 9001:2015 and the terms found in ISO 9000:2015.

There are three areas of significance found in ISO 9000:2015.

The first has been briefly outlined in the previous paragraphs. This standard contains a narrative of the nature and value of a QMS. ISO 9001:2015 says *what* you must do; ISO 9000:2015 says *why* you must do it.

Building on the "why" brings us to the second important section of ISO 9000:2015—the articulation of the seven quality management principles (QMPs). These principles are not requirements. Rather, they should be considered as guiding stars. They show the way. In a well-implemented QMS these stars shine through.

The seven QMPs have been around as long as ISO 9001 itself. They lay the foundation for the QMS. You may recall that there were originally eight principles. The technical experts who revised ISO 9001 decided that it would be of greater value to combine two of them—process approach and systems approach to management.

They are both now subsumed under the heading of "process approach." ISO 9000:2015 defines a process as "… [A] set of interrelated or interacting activities that use inputs to deliver an intended result." The QMPs state that the processes should be managed within a coherent system.

The seven QMPs are:

- Customer focus
- Leadership
- Engagement of people
- Process approach
- Improvement
- Evidence-based decision making
- Relationship management

Although no one principle is more important than the others, they do follow a logical progression.

The focus of ISO 9001:2015 is fulfilling customer requirements and enhancing customer satisfaction. The mission and policy that will enable this goal are established by the organization's leadership. They ensure that people are aware of and engaged in the mission to fulfill customer requirements and are provided with the resources and work environment that enable their effective participation. Individuals perform their functions within a controlled system that embraces the process approach. To continue to fulfill its mission, the organization operates in a culture that fosters continual improvement—through leadership, consistent engagement of its people, and utilizing evidence that enables good decision making. Finally, the organization ensures that it manages relationships (especially with providers) so that relevant interested parties can fulfill customer requirements.

For each of the quality management principles, ISO 9000:2015 provides a statement, a rationale, a list of potential benefits, and examples of activities relating to each of the principles.

The third section of ISO 9000:2015 that is of interest to users of ISO 9001:2015 contains the terms. At this point, it's important to point out that in section 2, ISO 9001:2015 specifically states that ISO 9000:2015 is the normative reference. This means that ISO 9000:2015 is indispensable for the application of ISO 9001:2015.

This is of particular importance because of the introduction of new terms and concepts in ISO 9001:2015. You can't fully understand the requirements if you don't understand the meaning of the terms.

The most important of the new terms have already been covered in chapters 1 and 2. They include:

- Context of the organization
- Risk
- Products and services
- Interested parties
- External provider
- Documented information

There are more than 150 terms found in ISO 9000:2015. They have differing degrees of relevance for various organizations. Because ISO 9000:2015 is also the normative reference for other ISO documents, it includes terms that aren't necessarily found in ISO 9001:2015. Some of these—innovation and efficiency, for example—can be helpful for organizations regardless of whether they constitute actual requirements within a QMS.

ISO 9000:2015 is important for three reasons. As stated, this document is indispensable for the application of ISO 9001:2015. It describes the fundamentals for your QMS, it enumerates the quality management principles that underlie a robust system, and it contains the terms required to fully understand the requirements of ISO 9001:2015.

Chapter 4

Changes by the Numbers

What follows is an overview of each of the major sections of ISO 9001:2015 with descriptions of changes, additions, and enhancements. It provides a summary of the requirements, but it does not cover all the requirements for each clause or subclause. The details for each can be found in the work sheets in part II of the book. Also, some of the requirements warrant more in-depth explanations. These are found in chapter 2. As they arise in this chapter, the text directs you back to chapter 2.

INTRODUCTION

The introduction and first two sections of ISO 9001:2015 have a lot of basic, boilerplate information. Some of the language is similar to text in ISO 9001:2008.

The introduction provides a narrative about the purpose of the document, the benefits that can be derived, and how the standard can be utilized. It reiterates use of the process approach and the plan-do-check-act (PDCA) cycle and introduces two models that are relevant to a holistic understanding of the document's structure and purpose. It provides a brief listing of the seven quality management principles, introduces the concept of risk-based thinking, mentions ISO 9001:2015's annexes, and discusses the relationship of ISO 9001:2015 to other management system standards and documents.

1—THE SCOPE

This is a brief statement of the scope of requirements within the standard. Similar to previous revisions, it defines the scope of the quality management system (QMS) as that which is needed to demonstrate "…[A]bility to consistently provide products and services that meet customer and applicable statutory and regulatory requirements… and to enhance customer satisfaction through the effective application of the system…"

2—NORMATIVE REFERENCES

This is where the statement is made that ISO 9000:2015 is the normative reference for ISO 9001:2015. Again, as stated in chapter 3, it means that ISO 9000:2015 is indispensable for the application of ISO 9001:2015.

3—TERMS AND DEFINITIONS

Although section 3 may seem redundant, there are some standards that have both normative references and additional terms that are specific to the standard. This isn't the case with ISO 9001:2015, so this section isn't as superfluous as it may seem. The absence of additional terms in ISO 9001:2015 means that any you might need are found in ISO 9000:2015.

4—CONTEXT OF THE ORGANIZATION

There are four important points in this section. The first two have been covered in greater detail in chapter 2: the need to identify internal and external issues that affect your organization's ability to achieve intended results, and the need to understand the needs and expectation of relevant interested parties.

The other two general requirements in this category are similar to ISO 9001:2008 with some subtle additions.

ISO 9001:2008 requires that the organization determine the boundaries and applicability of its QMS. If an organization has multiple divisions, it can choose to limit the scope to only specific divisions. This is not the same as the applicability of requirements. An organization may not define its scope to omit required processes. However, if it has four product lines, it can select to have only one within its scope. For example, there are three off-the-shelf product lines and one for highly specialized custom-designed products. The organization could choose to ignore the off-the-shelf lines and limit the scope to the custom stuff. This has to be scrupulously defined and controlled. Considering the tremendous overlaps with some processes, the confusion this could cause individuals internally, and the potential for lapses, it's not an advisable approach unless it's a smart business decision. Most organizations define the scope of their QMS as relating to all the processes that allow them to consistently produce all of the products in their portfolio.

The scope is comprised of two components: products and services and the processes relevant to achieving the organization's goals. The scope should be determined with appropriate consideration given to customers and their requirements, applicable statutory and regulatory requirements, influence of internal and external issues, and influence of relevant interested parties.

The other requirement in this clause is the need to establish the QMS. There's language about the deliberations and actions that are entailed in this process. If you're planning to transition to ISO 9001:2015, it's evident that you've covered this requirement and any further discussion is moot.

5—LEADERSHIP

There isn't much new in this section. The title has changed from "Management responsibility" to "Leadership," which is in better alignment with the quality management principles. There are amplified and enhanced requirements relating to management's role and responsibilities. Of particular note is the inclusion of requirements for ensuring that the QMS requirements are integrated into business processes and specifically ensuring that the QMS achieves its intended results. These enhancements highlight the importance of top management's engagement in the QMS.

The standard has clearer language concerning the communication of the quality policy. The concept and requirements for the management representative have been changed resulting in a heightened level of responsibility for top management on the one hand, but allowing for greater sharing of those responsibilities on the other.

Except for other small changes, this clause is similar to section 5 in ISO 9001:2008.

6—PLANNING

Planning used to be encompassed under the top management section with additional language about planning also found in other sections, such as the requirements relating to planning for what was formerly called "product realization."

There are several additions relating to planning. First, this is where the requirements for addressing risk are articulated. The standard directs users back to section 4 to the requirements relating to internal and external issues, and needs and expectations of interested parties to drive actions and decisions around both risk and opportunity.

Section 6 includes requirements relating to addressing risks and opportunities that were previously discussed in chapter 2. There's fairly prescriptive language about ensuring integration of the changes into the QMS and evaluating the effect of actions taken. Basically, how will you know if you've mitigated a risk or benefitted from an improvement?

Two additional enhancements have also been previously covered in chapter 2. They relate to the quality objectives and to planning and managing change.

7—SUPPORT

This section combines requirements that were found in multiple different sections of ISO 9001:2008. All of the support processes and resources are now included in section 7. General headings include people, infrastructure, environment for the operation of processes, monitoring and measuring resources, organizational knowledge, communication, awareness, competence, and documented information.

Documented information was discussed in chapter 2, which also discusses the diminished prescriptive requirements around infrastructure.

The word "training" is no longer in any of the headings, emphasizing the fact that there are other methods of achieving competence besides training. Language around awareness and competence is relatively unchanged.

ISO 9001:2015 introduces the new concept of "organizational knowledge." Briefly, this requires an organization to ensure that knowledge which isn't necessarily found in procedures or training manuals is maintained and accessible. The intent is to ensure that the information can be shared and transferred. Implementation of the requirements of this clause might also focus on the need to address the knowledge gap when someone retires or leaves the organization. Reflecting on the placement of this new concept, it's clear that organizational knowledge is a resource that may be looked upon as an organizational asset with value and risks if it's not properly maintained. The question to ask is: How will this knowledge be captured and retained? Organizations must also assess the eventuality that additional knowledge may be required to address changes in the organization or in the marketplace.

A subclause has been added that relates specifically to people. It's very basic and simply states that the organization shall provide the necessary persons for the effective implementation of the QMS.

Environment for the operation of processes is the old "work environment" requirement with an additional note for guidance.

The monitoring and measuring resources are expanded to ensure inclusion of methods and resources used for monitoring. Whereas the previous requirements were weighted heavily on manufacturing measurement and, hence, calibration, ISO 9001:2015 incorporates measurement options that address nonmanufacturing processes. Although this is particularly helpful to service and other nonmanufacturing organizations, it nevertheless provides guidance for monitoring of a variety of processes—for example, cycle-time calculations or service call duration—for all users.

Requirements relating specifically to calibration or "measurement traceability" are by and large unchanged from previous versions of ISO 9001.

Finally, there's a greatly elaborated subclause on communication. There's fairly specific language relating to what is to be communicated, when and how the communication will occur, and who will be communicating to whom.

8—OPERATION

Section 8 is essentially the product realization part of ISO 9001:2008

This section probably has fewer significant changes than any other. There are a lot of small changes and enhancements, but no new major concepts.

It begins with requirements for planning and control. This is followed by requirements relating to products and services. The requirements have been shuffled so that customer communication comes first with a few additional bullets. The rest of the text relating to determining and reviewing requirements (which many people still refer to as "contract review") is unchanged.

Design and development has had a makeover. The requirements have a more logical flow and seem to be more accommodating of the fact that this process is performed in very different ways by organizations. Some language—"standards or codes of practice," for example—refers to the design of services.

Purchasing is now called "control of externally provided processes, products and services." It encompasses three categories of supplier relationships: purchases from traditional suppliers; outsourced processes; and products, processes, and services provided by another supplier directly to the customer.

Most of the supplier qualification and purchasing requirements are unchanged. The relocation of outsourced processes to the "purchasing" subclause—although mostly unchanged—is more reflective of the facts that these processes are typically handled through the purchasing function. The third category is new and addresses an existing gap. The standard now provides specific requirements when a supplier ships product directly to the customer. This is typically referred to as "drop shipping" and is an efficient time-saving practice. Language relating to communications with suppliers and purchasing documents is relatively unchanged.

Production and service provisions have small changes and additions, but overall the requirements are the same. Requirements for identification and traceability are similarly unchanged. The subclause on property belonging to a customer now includes the provision for property belonging to external providers (suppliers). This takes into account the many instances in which supplier property (consigned inventory) is located at the organization's location.

Requirements for preservation of product are unchanged.

There is an additional subclause on post-delivery activities. This had been subsumed under the general requirements for the control of production processes. Breaking it out makes it more obvious to the small subset of organizations to whom this requirement applies.

There's a new subclause on control of changes. This serves to reinforce requirements from previous subclauses relative to the organization's need to control change. Here the requirement focuses on operational activities. An example might be a change to a manufacturing work order or change in a service contract during an installation.

The requirements for release of product had formerly been found under a subsequent clause dealing with monitoring and measuring of product. This is a logical and helpful relocation. It aligns with the process approach and makes a clear connection between the production of a product or service and the verification of the fulfillment of all requisite requirements.

The last section deals with controlling nonconforming outputs. For manufacturing activities, the requirements are only moderately changed. The other modifications relate to nonmanufacturing environments wherein controlling a nonconforming service might mean suspension of activities. There's some flexibility in how the product is controlled, but overall the requirements are the same as in ISO 9001:2008.

9—PERFORMANCE EVALUATION

This section combines the old clause 8.4 along with a few other requirements from the old (ISO 9001:2008) section 8 and the migration of management review from the old section 5.

The following clauses have only minor changes, and are for the most part similar or identical to ISO 9001:2008: analysis and evaluation, customer satisfaction, and internal audit. There is more prescriptive language about evaluating results of actions to address risks and opportunities and if planning has been effectively implemented. Because monitoring and measuring as well as analysis are based upon the organization's determination of what data needs to be monitored, there is some discretion in how this group of requirements is applied.

The only substantial change is the relocation of management review to this part of the standard. It's a logical and helpful change. Formerly, analysis of data requirements were found in the last clause, whereas management review was situated in an earlier clause. There was little relationship between the two. There was a disconnect between the two sets of requirements that seriously affected the effective implementation of both.

Now, the performance evaluation directly precedes the management review, providing the inputs necessary for informed decision making.

There's a new and subtle addition early in the management review subclause. It states that management review shall be planned. This may sound like a negligible change, but it lays the foundation for management to take a more active role in deciding what will be the subject of the review.

The requirements relating to the review are more logically organized, providing for a more holistic review with clearer perception of interdependencies and interrelations. Many are now grouped under an informal heading of trends.

There are additional requirements relating to the review of external provider performance, actions to address risk, adequacy of resources, and the extent to which quality objectives have been met.

10—IMPROVEMENT

The requirements in this section are for the most part unchanged, with the notable exception of the omission of preventive action. There's better linkage between nonconformance and the need to take action, including—when appropriate—corrective action. The language around corrective action includes a few minor additions that have always made sense, such as ensuring that appropriate changes are made to the QMS when action is taken.

The requirements end with continual improvement. This clause provides guidance on the inputs into management review and specifically makes mention of the fact that needs and opportunities may be addressed through the implementation of continual improvement.

Chapter 5

How to Use Part II of This Book

Now that you've plowed through part I, it's time to assess what needs to be done. What you're going to do next amounts to a gap analysis. You'll look at each requirement of the revised standard and determine:

- If your system complies with the current requirements of ISO 9001:2008*
- If your system conforms to the requirements of ISO 9001:2015
- What documented information or method you use to define and control the process and/or requirement. (This provides the evidence to substantiate your compliance.)
- What requirements are nonexistent in your system or need modification to conform to ISO 9001:2015.

*Note: If there are lapses in the current system, correction or corrective action should be implemented. In many cases, the actions can be rolled into the transition process, which may provide you the opportunity to solve a persistent problem through implementation of new or enhanced ISO 9001 requirements.

Part II has work sheets for each of the clauses and subclauses of ISO 9001:2015. The work sheets have a brief comment concerning the requirements including, in some cases, a comparison to ISO 9001:2008. The entire text of the requirements is not included and users are directed to refer to ISO 9001:2015. Additionally, ISO 9001:2015 contains guidance notes that will facilitate comprehension of the intent of the requirements and provide useful examples.

In instances where the requirements are unchanged, the text will be presented in italics. Italicized text denotes no change in requirements. This doesn't mean that the text is identical to ISO 9001:2008. There may be instances in which small editorial changes were made for the purpose of clarification. However, the requirement itself is unchanged.

For each individual work sheet, determine what documented information covers the requirement. Write the number of the document (if applicable) on the work sheet. For areas such as inspection or production it's OK to list the cluster or range (e.g., SOP 309–321). Bear in mind that the documented information may be in an ERP system, in CAD files, on the website, in a production router, or any other array of media. Remember that sometimes requirements are defined in "known good samples" or visual aids.

Finally, ISO 9001:2015 has no requirements for "documented procedures." It also does not have prescriptive requirements relating to what you must document. The requirement is to have "documented information determined by the organization as being necessary for the effectiveness of the quality management system." If you determine that a document is unnecessary, then that's what should be indicated on the work sheet.

The intent is to determine if a process is adequately defined and controlled. There's more latitude—more opportunity to define and implement your system in a manner that makes sense to you.

This isn't the time to try and resolve issues. Planning, revisions, documentation, and implementation will come later. If you want to ensure that you don't forget something, make brief notes on the back of the work sheet. This exercise is intended to streamline the process by isolating those features that require attention. In so doing, you will have less "stuff" diffusing your focus, allowing you to proceed with the implementation more efficiently.

After you have completed all the work sheets, divide them into three categories:

- *No further action is necessary.* The feature or activity complies with requirements of both ISO 9001:2008 and ISO 9001:2015.

- *Nonconformances occurring in your existing system that need to be addressed through your corrective action process.* These are nonconformances that should have been detected through your internal auditing process or some other monitoring mechanism. Although you may incorporate them into the transition project, it's important to note that they aren't new—you should have been fulfilling the requirement all along.

- *Features that need to be added, modified, or enhanced:* These are the actual tasks for your transition project. They will differ for each organization because many of the enhancements are good business practices that companies have initiated before ISO:9001:2015 was released. The other factors that will affect how many work sheets you have in this pile include the complexity of your processes and the number of requirements you determine as not being applicable to your QMS.

There are 64 work sheets. If you have a well-implemented quality system, it's likely that you won't have more than 20–25 sheets in the third pile. Of those, some may simply involve amending documentation to include a requirement that you've instituted as a matter of course because it's a good business practice that you never defined. There are a few—such as the requirements relating to risk-based thinking and understanding the context of the organization—that will automatically warrant some level of training.

Take the work sheets from the "no further action is necessary" pile and file them for safekeeping. As the project moves forward it may become necessary to revisit them, as they relate to the interaction with the processes you are adding or changing. Although these should be handled through your process for initiating changes and revising documents, it's acceptable to acknowledge that they do arise from the need to transition to the new standard.

Take the work sheets from the "nonconformance" pile and decide if:

- You should initiate corrective action
- It is a minor issue that can be handled with a quick fix
- It is closely related to something new in the standard and would be more efficiently addressed as part of the transition.

The work sheets from the third pile (along with any nonconformances that you have decided to address as part of the project) define the scope of your ISO 9001:2015 transition tasks.

In some instances, a change or addition is so minor that it's described only in the text box at the top of the work sheet. For other sheets, you should refer back to chapters 2 and 4 where the requirements are explained.

It's a good idea to schedule a management meeting after you have finished sorting the work sheets. This will give managers an opportunity to assess the resources required. Managers will also be active participants in developing the plan for the project. It will provide you a captive audience for assigning tasks and setting timetables.

Finally, this strategy fosters the adoption of the quality management principles: customer focus, leadership, engagement of people, process approach, improvement, evidence-based decision making, and relationship management. Fulfilling the requirements for transition should be perceived and recorded as a continual improvement initiative.

This book doesn't recommend any particular method, scheme, or approach for the project. Every organization is different. The scope of the transition project, the current status of your QMS, the level of urgency, and the availability of personnel all contribute to how your plans are implemented. Choose the strategy, sequence, and schedule that work best for you.

Communicate with your certification body (registrar) about the transition timetable. But remember, the clock is ticking. To prevent a lapse in your certification, you must have your assessment audit before September 2018.

Notes

_____

_____

_____

_____

_____

_____

_____

_____

_____

_____

_____

_____

_____

_____

_____

_____

_____

GAP ANALYSIS WORK SHEET 4.1

ISO 9001:2015 Reference	Comments
4.1 Understanding the organization and its context	Internal and external issues may relate to a variety of factors that may be specific to the organization. Examples of internal issues include: staffing levels, succession planning, capacity, process changes, or development of a new product. External issues might relate to changes in the marketplace, financial policies, cash flow, availability of raw materials, political upheaval, or regulatory requirements. These may change over time and must be monitored.

Requirement	How defined/documented and controlled?	Need to implement	Needs work/ revision	OK
Determine internal and external issues relevant to organization's purpose.				
Monitor issues.				

Notes

Notes

GAP ANALYSIS WORK SHEET 4.2

ISO 9001:2015 Reference	Comments
4.2 Understanding the needs and expectations of interested parties	According to ISO 9000:2015, interested parties are those who can affect, be affected by, or perceive themselves to be affected by actions and decisions. They can be both internal and external. Typical examples include customers, suppliers, employees, stockholders, or the community. Because things change, information must be monitored.

Requirement	How defined/documented and controlled?	Need to implement	Needs work/ revision	OK
Determine interested parties who are relevant to organization's purpose.				
Monitor information about them.				

Notes

Notes

GAP ANALYSIS WORK SHEET 4.3

ISO 9001:2015 Reference	Comments
4.3 Determining the scope of the quality management system	The scope of the QMS includes the boundaries of the system and products and services covered. A statement of the scope would include any justification for requirements of the standard that are not applicable to the organization. It needs to be maintained as documented information. This is similar to ISO 9001:2008 with small changes and additions. Information from clauses 4.1 and 4.2 facilitate determining the scope of the organization.

Requirement	How defined/documented and controlled?	Need to implement	Needs work/ revision	OK
Determine scope, boundaries, and applicability of the QMS.				
Maintain documented information.				

Notes

Notes

GAP ANALYSIS WORK SHEET 4.4

ISO 9001:2015 Reference	Comments
4.4 Quality management system and its processes	This is relatively unchanged from ISO 9001:2008. Determine the processes (including sequence and interaction), method of monitoring performance indicators, resources required, and responsibility. There's added language about determining risk and opportunities. *Italicized text denotes no change in requirements.*

Requirement	How defined/documented and controlled?	Need to implement	Needs work/ revision	OK
Determine processes and their inputs and expected outputs.				
Determine the sequence and interaction of processes.				
Determine and apply methods for monitoring performance indicators.				
Determine the resources needed.				
Assign responsibility and authority.				
Address risks and opportunities.				
Maintain documented information to support operation.				

Notes

Notes

GAP ANALYSIS WORK SHEET 5.1.1

ISO 9001:2015 Reference	Comments
5.1.1 Leadership and commitment—General	This subclause includes additional and more specific requirements focused on top management. Much of this is probably implemented if the QMS is established. *Italicized text denotes no change in requirements.*

Requirement	How defined/documented and controlled?	Need to implement	Needs work/ revision	OK
Take accountability for effectiveness of the QMS.				
Ensure that the quality policy and quality objectives are established.				
Ensure the integration of QMS requirements into organization's business processes.				
Promote use of the process approach and risk-based thinking.				
Ensure resources are available.				
Communicate the importance of effective quality management.				
Ensure the QMS achieves its intended results.				
Engage, direct, and support persons who contribute to the QMS.				
Promote improvement.				

Notes

Notes

GAP ANALYSIS WORK SHEET 5.1.2

ISO 9001:2015 Reference	Comments
5.1.2	There are small additions to the requirements relating to customer focus.
Customer focus	*Italicized text denotes no change in requirements.*

Requirement	How defined/documented and controlled?	Need to Implement	Needs work/ revision	OK
Ensure customer and applicable statutory and regulatory requirements are determined, understood, and met.				
Address risks and opportunities that affect ability to meet customer requirements.				
Retain organizational focus on enhancing customer satisfaction.				

Notes

Notes

GAP ANALYSIS WORK SHEET 5.2.1

ISO 9001:2015 Reference	Comments
5.2.1	There are some additions to the quality policy requirements.
Establishing the quality policy	*Italicized text denotes no change in requirements.*

Requirement	How defined/documented and controlled?	Need to implement	Needs work/ revision	OK
Quality policy must be: • *Appropriate to the purpose and context of the organization*				
• Support its strategic direction				
• Include a commitment to satisfy applicable requirements				
• *Provide for quality objectives*				
• *Includes commitment to continually improve QMS*				

Notes

Notes

GAP ANALYSIS WORK SHEET 5.2.2

ISO 9001:2015 Reference	Comments
5.2.2	There is one significant addition.
Communicating the quality policy	*Italicized text denotes no change in requirements.*

Requirement	How defined/documented and controlled?	Need to implement	Needs work/ revision	OK
Quality policy must be: • *Communicated and understood*				
• *Available and maintained*				
• Available to relevant interested parties				

Notes

Notes

GAP ANALYSIS WORK SHEET 5.3

ISO 9001:2015 Reference	Comments
5.3 Organizational roles, responsibilities, and authorities	Much of these requirements remain unchanged with one addition and the notable exception previously discussed relating to the role of the management representative with the implication that responsibility may be shared. *Italicized text denotes no change in requirements.*

Requirement	How defined/documented and controlled?	Need to implement	Needs work/ revision	OK
Responsibility must be assigned, communicated, and understood. Responsibility shall be assigned for: • *Ensuring QMS conforms to requirements*				
• Ensuring that the processes deliver their intended outputs				
• *Reporting on the performance of QMS*				
• *Promotion of customer focus throughout the organization*				
• *Ensuring the integrity of the QMS is maintained when changes are planned and implemented*				

Notes

Notes

GAP ANALYSIS WORK SHEET 6.1.1

ISO 9001:2015 Reference	Comments
6.1.1	This is the first part of the planning clause, where the concept of risk is most explicitly
Planning—Actions to address risks and opportunities	defined in terms of requirements. However, it's clear that the requirements have broad applicability throughout the standard. The only similarity to ISO 9001:2008 is the retention of some of the language used to describe preventive action.

Requirement	How defined/documented and controlled?	Need to implement	Needs work/ revision	OK
When planning, consider issues in clauses 4.1 and 4.2 that need to be addressed to:				
• Enhance desirable effects				
• Prevent or reduce problems or other undesirable issues				
• Achieve improvement				

Notes

Notes

GAP ANALYSIS WORK SHEET 6.1.2

ISO 9001:2015 Reference	Comments
6.1.2	This second part of the subclause has more specific information about how to plan, including ensuring that actions are integrated and implemented into the QMS and how to evaluate the effectiveness of actions taken.
Planning—Actions to address risks and opportunities	

Requirement	How defined/documented and controlled?	Need to implement	Needs work/ revision	OK
When planning, include: • How the plans will be implemented into the QMS				
• How the effectiveness will be assessed				

Notes

Notes

GAP ANALYSIS WORK SHEET 6.2.1

ISO 9001:2015 Reference	Comments
6.2.1 Quality objectives— Establishing	These requirements are comparable to the ones found in ISO 9001:2008 with minor additions. *Italicized text denotes no change in requirements.*

Requirement	How defined/documented and controlled?	Need to implement	Needs work/ revision	OK
Objectives must be: • *Consistent with quality policy and measurable*				
• *Consider requirements*				
• Relevant to product and enhancement of customer satisfaction				
• Monitored				
• Communicated				
• Updated as needed				

Notes

Notes

GAP ANALYSIS WORK SHEET 6.2.2

ISO 9001:2015 Reference	Comments
6.2.2	These requirements are new. They require that organizations plan for how to achieve quality objectives.
Quality objectives— Planning for achievement	

Requirement	How defined/documented and controlled?	Need to implement	Needs work/ revision	OK
Planning:				
• What to do				
• Resources required				
• Responsibility				
• When completed				
• How results will be evaluated				

Notes

Notes

GAP ANALYSIS WORK SHEET 6.3

ISO 9001:2015 Reference	Comments
6.3	These requirements are new. The need to control change has always been implied. In ISO 9001:2015, the requirements are explicit.
Planning of changes	

Requirement	How defined/documented and controlled?	Need to implement	Needs work/ revision	OK
As part of planning, consider:				
• Purpose and potential consequences				
• Maintaining integrity of the QMS				
• Resources				
• Responsibility and authority				
• How results will be evaluated				

Notes

Notes

GAP ANALYSIS WORK SHEET 7.1.1

ISO 9001:2015 Reference	Comments
7.1.1	This is a broad overview of the requirements that are detailed in subsequent subclauses. It requires the provision of resources for the implementation and maintenance of the QMS and for improvement. The need to obtain resources from external providers can link to requirements for outsourced processes in section 8.
Support—General	

Requirement	How defined/documented and controlled?	Need to implement	Needs work/ revision	OK
Determine and provide required resources.				
Consider: • Capability and constraints on existing resources				
• Need to obtain resources from external providers				

Notes

Notes

GAP ANALYSIS WORK SHEET 7.1.2

ISO 9001:2015 Reference	Comments
7.1.2	This is a brief statement that links to later requirements relating to competence and awareness. This subclause basically requires provision of the persons required for implementation of QMS and operation and control of processes.
Support—People	

Requirement	How defined/documented and controlled?	Need to implement	Needs work/ revision	OK
Provide necessary persons for implementation of the QMS and operation and control of processes.				

Notes

Notes

GAP ANALYSIS WORK SHEET 7.1.3

ISO 9001:2015 Reference	Comments
7.1.3 Support—Infrastructure	The requirements in this subclause are changed from ISO 9001:2008 in that they have been migrated into a note. However, because the overall requirement is to provide and maintain the necessary infrastructure, the guidance found in the note will align with currently implemented requirements, resulting in essentially no change.

Requirement	How defined/documented and controlled?	Need to implement	Needs work/ revision	OK
Provide and maintain the necessary infrastructure to achieve product conformance.				

Notes

Notes

GAP ANALYSIS WORK SHEET 7.1.4

ISO 9001:2015 Reference	Comments
7.1.4 Support—Environment for the operation of processes	This subclause is basically the same as the "work environment" clause from ISO 9001:2008. There are subtle changes in text that differentiate between operation of processes and achieving conformity of products and services. The note provides ample guidance with examples relating to both.

Requirement	How defined/documented and controlled?	Need to implement	Needs work/ revision	OK
Determine, provide, and maintain the necessary environment.				

Notes

Notes

GAP ANALYSIS WORK SHEET 7.1.5.1

ISO 9001:2015 Reference	Comments
7.1.5.1 Monitoring and measuring resources—General	This subclause and the next (7.1.5.2) are essentially the same as the old requirements for control of monitoring and measuring equipment. There are changes in language to be more inclusive of service organizations and others whose measurements don't fit into the previously more manufacturing-focused paradigm.

Requirement	How defined/documented and controlled?	Need to implement	Needs work/ revision	OK
Determine resources needed for valid and reliable monitoring and measuring.				
Ensure suitability.				
Ensure continuing fitness for purpose through maintenance.				
Retain records of fitness for purpose.				

Notes

Notes

GAP ANALYSIS WORK SHEET 7.1.5.2

ISO 9001:2015 Reference	Comments
7.1.5.2 Measurement traceability	This subclause is similar to previous requirements in ISO 9001:2008 that have often been associated with calibration and similar control of measuring devices. There are subtle changes to clarify requirements. Overall requirements are unchanged. *Italicized text denotes no change in requirements.*

Requirement	How defined/documented and controlled?	Need to implement	Needs work/ revision	OK
Equipment calibrated or verified				
Identified/status known				
Safeguarded from adjustments and deterioration				
Determine validity of previous measurements when measuring equipment is found to be unfit and take appropriate action.				

Notes

Notes

GAP ANALYSIS WORK SHEET 7.1.6

ISO 9001:2015 Reference	Comments
7.1.6	This is a new concept and a new requirement. It addresses experience, lessons
Organizational knowledge	learned, undocumented knowledge, and intellectual property.

Requirement	How defined/documented and controlled?	Need to implement	Needs work/ revision	OK
Determine the knowledge necessary for operation of processes and to achieve product conformance.				
Maintain organizational knowledge.				
When addressing change, assess current knowledge and how to acquire needed additional knowledge.				

Notes

Notes

GAP ANALYSIS WORK SHEET 7.2

ISO 9001:2015 Reference	Comments
7.2	The language in this subclause is almost identical to ISO 9001:2008.
Competence	*Italicized text denotes no change in requirements.*

Requirement	How defined/documented and controlled?	Need to implement	Needs work/ revision	OK
Determine the necessary competence of person(s) doing work that affects the QMS.				
Ensure persons are competent.				
Take actions to acquire competence and evaluate effectiveness.				
Retain appropriate documented information.				

Notes

Notes

_____

_____

_____

_____

_____

_____

_____

_____

_____

_____

_____

_____

_____

_____

_____

_____

GAP ANALYSIS WORK SHEET 7.3

ISO 9001:2015 Reference	Comments
7.3	This language is similar to ISO 9001:2008 but has additional requirements.
Awareness	*Italicized text denotes no change in requirements.*

Requirement	How defined/documented and controlled?	Need to implement	Needs work/ revision	OK
Awareness of: • *Quality policy* • Relevant quality objectives • Contribution to the QMS and benefits of improvement • Implications of not conforming with QMS requirements				

Notes

Notes

GAP ANALYSIS WORK SHEET 7.4

ISO 9001:2015 Reference	Comments
7.4	These requirements relate to internal and external communications.
Communication	

Requirement	How defined/documented and controlled?	Need to implement	Needs work/ revision	OK
What will be communicated				
When to communicate				
Who communicates and with whom				
How to communicate				

Notes

Notes

GAP ANALYSIS WORK SHEET 7.5.1

ISO 9001:2015 Reference	Comments
7.5.1 Documented information—General	These are general requirements for documented information. They are relatively unchanged from ISO 9001:2008 with the notable exception that documents and records are now subsumed under the heading of documented information. *Italicized text denotes no change in requirements.*

Requirement	How defined/documented and controlled?	Need to implement	Needs work/ revision	OK
QMS shall include: • *Documented information required by ISO 9001:2015*				
• *Documented information necessary for effectiveness of the QMS*				

Notes

Notes

_____

_____

_____

_____

_____

_____

_____

_____

_____

_____

_____

_____

_____

_____

_____

_____

GAP ANALYSIS WORK SHEET 7.5.2

ISO 9001:2015 Reference	Comments
7.5.2 Documented information— Creating and updating	It's important to remember that the requirements related to all documented information were formerly referred to as documents and records. There are small enhancements in requirements. *Italicized text denotes no change in requirements.*

Requirement	How defined/documented and controlled?	Need to implement	Needs work/ revision	OK
When creating and updating, ensure: • Appropriate identification and description				
• Appropriate format				
• *Review and approval for suitability and adequacy*				

Notes

Notes

GAP ANALYSIS WORK SHEET 7.5.3.1

ISO 9001:2015 Reference	Comments
7.5.3.1	These requirements relate to availability, maintenance, and protection.
Documented information—Control	*Italicized text denotes no change in requirements.*

Requirement	How defined/documented and controlled?	Need to implement	Needs work/ revision	OK
When controlling documented information, ensure: • Available and suitable where and when needed				
• Protected from loss, deterioration, or improper use				
• *Review and approval for suitability and adequacy*				

Notes

Notes

GAP ANALYSIS WORK SHEET 7.5.3.2

ISO 9001:2015 Reference	Comments
7.5.3.2 Documented information— Control	These requirements relate mostly to requirements that used to be associated with records. However, ISO 9001:2015 recognizes that some of the requirements are relevant to both documents and records, i.e., documented information. *Italicized text denotes no change in requirements.*

Requirement	How defined/documented and controlled?	Need to implement	Needs work/ revision	OK
When controlling documented information, address: • *Distribution, access, retrieval, use*				
• *Storage and preservation*				
• Control of changes				
• *Retention and disposition*				

Notes

Notes

GAP ANALYSIS WORK SHEET 8.1

ISO 9001:2015 Reference	Comments
8.1 Operational planning and control	These are similar to the general planning requirements for the former product realization requirement found in ISO 9001:2008. *Italicized text denotes no change in requirements.*

Requirement	How defined/documented and controlled?	Need to implement	Needs work/ revision	OK
When determining requirements for products and services, address: • *Establish criteria for processes and acceptance of products and services.*				
• *Determine resources needed.*				
• Control the processes in accordance with the criteria.				
• Determine and keep documented information to the extent necessary.				
Ensure output of planning is suitable for operations.				
Control changes and review consequences of unintended changes.				
Ensure control of outsourced processes.				

Notes

Notes

GAP ANALYSIS WORK SHEET 8.2.1

ISO 9001:2015 Reference	Comments
8.2.1	There are general requirements about communication in section 7. This relates specifically to communications with customers.
Customer communication	
	Italicized text denotes no change in requirements.

Requirement	How defined/documented and controlled?	Need to implement	Needs work/ revision	OK
Communications with customers: • Information about products				
• Inquiries, contract, orders, changes				
• *Feedback, including complaints*				
• Specific requirements for contingency actions, if relevant				

Notes

Notes

GAP ANALYSIS WORK SHEET 8.2.2

ISO 9001:2015 Reference	Comments
8.2.2 Determining the requirements for products and services	These requirements have been known since 1994 as "contract review." The requirements are relatively unchanged with one addition. *Italicized text denotes no change in requirements.*

Requirement	How defined/documented and controlled?	Need to implement	Needs work/ revision	OK
Determining requirements for products and services (including delivery and post-delivery activities), ensure: • *Requirements are defined.*				
• *Applicable statutory and regulatory requirements are considered.*				
• *Requirements determined necessary by the organization are considered.*				
• Organization can meet the claims for the products and services.				

Notes

Notes

GAP ANALYSIS WORK SHEET 8.2.3.1

ISO 9001:2015 Reference	Comments
8.2.3.1 Review of requirements for products and services	These requirements have been known since 1994 as "contract review." The requirements are relatively unchanged with one addition. Unlike ISO 9001:2008, some of the requirements are reiterated from the previous subclause. *Italicized text denotes no change in requirements.*

Requirement	How defined/documented and controlled?	Need to implement	Needs work/ revision	OK
Ensure ability to meet requirements.				
Conduct review before committing to supply products and services, including: • *Requirements not stated by customer, but necessary for intended use*				
• Contract or order requirements differing from those previously expressed				
• *Applicable statutory and regulatory requirements*				
• Requirements specified by the organization				
Contract requirements differing from those previously defined are resolved.				
Customer's requirements are confirmed before acceptance when no documented statement provided.				

Notes

Notes

GAP ANALYSIS WORK SHEET 8.2.3.2

ISO 9001:2015 Reference	Comments
8.2.3.2 Review of requirements— Documented information	These requirements state explicitly what information must be retained as the result of review or if there are any new product requirements. *Italicized text denotes no change in requirements.*

Requirement	How defined/documented and controlled?	Need to implement	Needs work/ revision	OK
Retain documented information concerning: • *Results of the review*				
• Any new product and service requirements				

Notes

Notes

GAP ANALYSIS WORK SHEET 8.2.4

ISO 9001:2015 Reference	Comments
8.2.4	This is a new requirement dealing with handling changes to requirements.
Changes to requirements for products and services	

Requirement	How defined/documented and controlled?	Need to implement	Needs work/ revision	OK
Documented information amended				
Relevant people informed of changed requirements.				

Notes

Notes

GAP ANALYSIS WORK SHEET 8.3.1

ISO 9001:2015 Reference	Comments
8.3.1 Design and development— General	This is an overall statement relating to the establishment, implementation, and maintenance of a design control process.

Requirement	How defined/documented and controlled?	Need to implement	Needs work/ revision	OK
Establish, implement, and maintain a design and development process.				

Notes

Notes

GAP ANALYSIS WORK SHEET 8.3.2

ISO 9001:2015 Reference	Comments
8.3.2	The requirements for planning are more prescriptive and detailed than in ISO 9001:2008. Some of the text is similar with several additional requirements.
Design and development planning	*Italicized text denotes no change in requirements.*

Requirement	How defined/documented and controlled?	Need to implement	Needs work/ revision	OK
When planning the design process consider: • Nature, duration, and complexity of design and development activities				
• *Required process stages, including reviews*				
• *Required verification and validation activities*				
• Responsibilities and authorities				
• Internal and external resources				
• Level of control expected for design and development process by customers and other relevant interested parties				
• *Need to control interfaces between persons involved in process*				
• Need for customer and user involvement in process				
• Requirements for subsequent provision of products and services				
• Documented information needed to demonstrate that design requirements have been met				

Notes

Notes

GAP ANALYSIS WORK SHEET 8.3.3

ISO 9001:2015 Reference	Comments
8.3.3	Design inputs are similar to ISO 9001:2008 with several additions.
Design and development inputs	*Italicized text denotes no change in requirements.*

Requirement	How defined/documented and controlled?	Need to implement	Needs work/ revision	OK
Inputs to be determined essential for specific types of products and services to be designed				
Organization shall consider: • *Functional and performance requirements*				
• *Statutory and regulatory requirements*				
• *Information derived from previous similar design activities*				
• Standards or codes of practice that the organization has committed to implement				
• Potential consequences of failure due to nature of products and services				
Inputs are adequate, complete, and unambiguous.				
Conflicts between inputs are resolved.				
Documented information is retained.				

Notes

Notes

GAP ANALYSIS WORK SHEET 8.3.4

ISO 9001:2015 Reference	Comments
8.3.4 Design and development controls	These requirements are similar to ISO 9001:2008 in that they reflect the same intent. However, the language is markedly changed and requirements have been shuffled and redistributed into different subclauses. *Italicized text denotes no change in requirements.*

Requirement	How defined/documented and controlled?	Need to implement	Needs work/ revision	OK
Design and development outputs to ensure: • Results to be achieved are defined.				
• Reviews are conducted to evaluate ability to meet requirements.				
• *Verification activities conducted ensuring resulting products and services meet requirements.*				
• *Validation activities are conducted ensuring requirements for application are met.*				
• *Any necessary actions are taken on problems determined during the reviews.*				
• *Documented information of these activities is retained.*				

Notes

Notes

GAP ANALYSIS WORK SHEET 8.3.5

ISO 9001:2015 Reference	Comments
8.3.5 Design and development outputs	These requirements are similar to ISO 9001:2008 in that they reflect the same intent. However, the language is markedly changed and requirements have been shuffled and redistributed into different subclauses. There are additional requirements. *Italicized text denotes no change in requirements.*

Requirement	How defined/documented and controlled?	Need to implement	Needs work/ revision	OK
Design and development outputs to ensure: • *Meet input requirements.*				
• Requirements are adequate for subsequent processes for provision of products and services.				
• Include or reference monitoring and measuring requirements and acceptance criteria				
• *Specify the characteristics of the products and services essential for their intended purpose and safe and proper provision.*				
Retain documented information of outputs.				

Notes

Notes

GAP ANALYSIS WORK SHEET 8.3.6

ISO 9001:2015 Reference	Comments
8.3.6 Design and development changes	The design change process has been rewritten. Requirements are substantively different from ISO 9001:2008. *Italicized text denotes no change in requirements.*

Requirement	How defined/documented and controlled?	Need to implement	Needs work/ revision	OK
Identify, review, and control changes made during or subsequent to design and development, to extent necessary to ensure that there is no adverse effect.				
Retain documented information on: • Design and development changes				
• *Results of reviews*				
• Authorization of changes				
• Actions taken to prevent adverse effects				

Notes

Notes

GAP ANALYSIS WORK SHEET 8.4.1

ISO 9001:2015 Reference	Comments
8.4.1 Control of externally provided processes, products, and services—General	These requirements were formerly under the purchasing clause. Requirements relating to outsourced processes have been combined under this clause along with new requirements. *Italicized text denotes no change in requirements.* *Note: For brevity in this work sheet, "product" refers to externally provided processes, products, and services.

Requirement	How defined/documented and controlled?	Need to implement	Needs work/ revision	OK
Ensure product* conforms to requirements.				
Determine the controls to be applied to products when: • *Products are intended for incorporation into the organization's products.*				
• Products are provided directly to the customer(s) by external providers on behalf of the organization.				
• Process, or part of a process, is provided by an external supplier.				
Determine and apply criteria for evaluation, selection, monitoring, and re-evaluation of external providers.				
Retain documented information of these activities and any necessary actions arising from the evaluations.				

Notes

Notes

GAP ANALYSIS WORK SHEET 8.4.2

ISO 9001:2015 Reference	Comments
8.4.2 Control of externally provided processes, products, and services— Type and extent of control	These requirements were formerly under the purchasing clause. Requirements relating to outsourced processes have been combined under this clause along with new requirements. *Italicized text denotes no change in requirements.* *Note: For brevity in this work sheet, "product" refers to externally provided processes, products, and services.

Requirement	How defined/documented and controlled?	Need to implement	Needs work/ revision	OK
Ensure that products* do not adversely affect the organization's ability to consistently deliver conforming products to customers.				
Ensure that externally provided processes remain within control of its QMS.				
Define controls to be applied to external provider and resulting output.				
Take into consideration: • Potential impact of products on organization's ability to meet customer and statutory and regulatory requirements				
• Effectiveness of the controls applied by the external provider				
Determine verification or other activities necessary to ensure that products meet requirements.				

Notes

Notes

GAP ANALYSIS WORK SHEET 8.4.3

ISO 9001:2015 Reference	Comments
8.4.3 Control of externally provided processes, products, and services— Information for external providers	These requirements were formerly under the purchasing clause. Requirements relating to outsourced processes have been combined under this clause along with new requirements. *Italicized text denotes no change in requirements.* *Note: For brevity in this work sheet, "product" refers to externally provided processes, products, and services.

Requirement	How defined/documented and controlled?	Need to implement	Needs work/ revision	OK
Ensure adequacy of requirements prior to communication to external provider				
Communicate to external providers its requirements for: • *Products* *				
• *Approval of products, methods, processes and equipment, and release of products*				
• *Competence and qualification of persons*				
• External providers' interactions with the organization				
• Control and monitoring of the external providers' performance to be applied by the organization				
• *Verification or validation activities that organization, or its customer, intends to perform at external providers' premises*				

Notes

Notes

GAP ANALYSIS WORK SHEET 8.5.1

ISO 9001:2015 Reference	Comments
8.5.1 Control of production and service provision	These requirements are similar to those found in ISO 9001:2008. There are minor changes and some additional requirements. *Italicized text denotes no change in requirements.*

Requirement	How defined/documented and controlled?	Need to implement	Needs work/ revision	OK
Implement production and service provision under controlled conditions.				
Controlled conditions include: • Availability of documented information that defines characteristics of the products, services, or the activities and results to be achieved				
• *Suitable monitoring and measuring resources*				
• *Competence and qualification of persons*				
• Appointment of competent persons				
• *Validation and periodic revalidation of processes where resulting output cannot be verified by subsequent monitoring or measurement*				
• Implementation of actions to prevent human error				
• *Implementation of release, delivery, and post-delivery activities*				

Notes

Notes

GAP ANALYSIS WORK SHEET 8.5.2

ISO 9001:2015 Reference	Comments
8.5.2 Identification and traceability	These requirements are comparable to those found in ISO 9001:2008. However, the language has changes that elaborate the requirements. *Italicized text denotes no change in requirements.*

Requirement	How defined/documented and controlled?	Need to implement	Needs work/ revision	OK
Use suitable means to identify outputs when necessary to ensure conformity of products and services.				
Identify status of outputs with respect to monitoring and measurement requirements throughout production and service provision.				
Control unique identification of the outputs when traceability is a requirement and retain documented information for traceability.				

Notes

Notes

GAP ANALYSIS WORK SHEET 8.5.3

ISO 9001:2015 Reference	Comments
8.5.3	The big change in the requirements for this subclause is that they now relate to both customer-owned and supplier-owned property. The specific requirements are comparable to ISO 9001:2008.
Property belonging to customers or external providers	

Requirement	How defined/documented and controlled?	Need to implement	Needs work/ revision	OK
Exercise care with property belonging to customers or external providers while it's under the organization's control.				
Identify, verify, protect, and safeguard customers' or external providers' property.				
When property is lost, damaged, or otherwise unsuitable for use, report to customer or external provider and retain documented information.				

Notes

Notes

GAP ANALYSIS WORK SHEET 8.5.4

ISO 9001:2015 Reference	Comments
8.5.4	Similar to ISO 9001:2008 with modifications to accommodate nonmanufacturing
Preservation	organizations.

Requirement	How defined/documented and controlled?	Need to implement	Needs work/ revision	OK
Preserve the outputs during production and service provision to the extent necessary to ensure conformity to requirements.				

Notes

Notes

GAP ANALYSIS WORK SHEET 8.5.5

ISO 9001:2015 Reference	Comments
8.5.5	This used to be a brief bullet point under subclause 7.5.1. It now has its own
Post-delivery activities	subclause with enhanced requirements.

Requirement	How defined/documented and controlled?	Need to implement	Needs work/ revision	OK
Consider and meet requirements as they relate to: • Statutory and regulatory requirements				
• Potential undesired consequences				
• Nature, use, and intended lifetime of product or service				
• Customer requirements and feedback				

Notes

Notes

GAP ANALYSIS WORK SHEET 8.5.6

ISO 9001:2015 Reference	Comments
8.5.6 Control of changes	These requirements are new to the extent that they explicitly link such processes as design changes and engineering changes to the production and service provision processes. They also ensure better control of changes that occur during the manufacturing process.

Requirement	How defined/documented and controlled?	Need to implement	Needs work/ revision	OK
Review and control changes for production or service provision to ensure continuing conformity with requirements.				
Retain documented information describing results of review of changes, the person(s) authorizing the change, and any necessary actions arising from review.				

Notes

Notes

GAP ANALYSIS WORK SHEET 8.6

ISO 9001:2015 Reference	Comments
8.6 Release of products and services	These requirements were formerly found in the sections on product acceptance and monitoring and measuring of product. *Italicized text denotes no change in requirements.*

Requirement	How defined/documented and controlled?	Need to implement	Needs work/ revision	OK
Implement planned arrangements at appropriate stages to verify that requirements have been met.				
Release of products and services not to proceed until the planned arrangements have been satisfactorily completed, unless otherwise approved by a relevant authority.				
Retain documented information on the release to include evidence of conformity with the acceptance criteria and traceability to the person(s) authorizing the release.				

Notes

Notes

GAP ANALYSIS WORK SHEET 8.7.1

ISO 9001:2015 Reference	Comments
8.7.1 Control of nonconforming outputs	There are multiple changes in the language relating to what was previously referred to as nonconforming product. It includes requirements specifically targeted to service provision.

Requirement	How defined/documented and controlled?	Need to implement	Needs work/ revision	OK
Ensure that nonconforming outputs are identified and controlled to prevent unintended use or delivery.				
Take appropriate action based on nature of nonconformity and effect on conformity of products and services. • Applies when detected after delivery of products, during, or after the provision of services.				
Deal with nonconforming outputs by: • Correction				
• Segregation, containment, return, or suspension of provision of products and services				
• Informing the customer				
• Obtaining authorization for acceptance under concession				
Verify conformity when nonconforming outputs corrected.				

Notes

Notes

GAP ANALYSIS WORK SHEET 8.7.2

ISO 9001:2015 Reference	Comments
8.7.2 Control of nonconforming outputs	These requirements address which documented information needs to be retained.

Requirement	How defined/documented and controlled?	Need to implement	Needs work/ revision	OK
Documented information to be retained. Description of: ● Nonconformity				
● Actions taken				
● Any concessions obtained				
● Authority deciding the action				

Notes

Notes

GAP ANALYSIS WORK SHEET 9.1.1

ISO 9001:2015 Reference	Comments
9.1.1 Monitoring, measurement, analysis, and evaluation—General	These requirements present an overview of the requirements that are the subject of the subsequent subclauses.

Requirement	How defined/documented and controlled?	Need to implement	Needs work/ revision	OK
Determine: • What needs to be monitored and measured				
• Methods				
• When performed				
• When results to be evaluated and analyzed				
Evaluate performance and effectiveness of the QMS.				
Retain documented information.				

Notes

Notes

GAP ANALYSIS WORK SHEET 9.1.2

ISO 9001:2015 Reference	Comments
9.1.2	These requirements relating to customer satisfaction are virtually unchanged.
Customer satisfaction	*Italicized text denotes no change in requirements.*

Requirement	How defined/documented and controlled?	Need to implement	Needs work/ revision	OK
Monitor customers' perceptions of the degree to which their needs and expectations have been fulfilled.				
Determine methods for obtaining, monitoring, and reviewing information.				

Notes

Notes

GAP ANALYSIS WORK SHEET 9.1.3

ISO 9001:2015 Reference	Comments
9.1.3	These requirements are similar to ISO 9001:2008, but there have been multiple additions.
Analysis and evaluation	

Requirement	How defined/documented and controlled?	Need to implement	Needs work/ revision	OK
Analyze and evaluate appropriate data and information arising from monitoring and measurement.				
Use results to evaluate:				
• Conformity of products and services				
• Degree of customer satisfaction				
• Performance and effectiveness of the QMS				
• Effectiveness of actions taken to address risks and opportunities				
• If planning has been implemented effectively				
• Performance of suppliers				
• Need to improve the QMS				

Notes

Notes

GAP ANALYSIS WORK SHEET 9.2.1

ISO 9001:2015 Reference	Comments
9.2.1	Requirements relating to internal audits are virtually unchanged.
Internal audit	*Italicized text denotes no change in requirements.*

Requirement	How defined/documented and controlled?	Need to implement	Needs work/ revision	OK
Conduct internal audits at planned intervals.				
Ensure conformance to: • *Organization's requirements for its QMS*				
• *Requirements of ISO 9001:2015*				
QMS effectively implemented and maintained.				

Notes

Notes

GAP ANALYSIS WORK SHEET 9.2.2

ISO 9001:2015 Reference	Comments
9.2.2 Internal audit	These requirements relating to internal audits are mostly unchanged except for the addition of language about responsibility, impartiality, and reporting to management. *Italicized text denotes no change in requirements.*

Requirement	How defined/documented and controlled?	Need to implement	Needs work/ revision	OK
Plan, establish, implement, and maintain an audit program including the frequency, methods, responsibilities, planning requirements, and reporting.				
Define the audit criteria and scope.				
Select auditors and conduct audits to ensure objectivity and the impartiality of the audit process.				
Ensure that the results of the audits are reported to relevant management.				
Take appropriate correction and corrective actions without undue delay.				
Retain documented information of audit results.				

Notes

Notes

GAP ANALYSIS WORK SHEET 9.3.1

ISO 9001:2015 Reference	Comments
9.3.1 Management review— General	This a general overview of the requirements for management review. There is new language relating to strategic direction.

Requirement	How defined/documented and controlled?	Need to implement	Needs work/ revision	OK
Review the QMS at planned intervals to ensure continuing suitability, adequacy, effectiveness, and alignment with the strategic direction.				

Notes

Notes

GAP ANALYSIS WORK SHEET 9.3.2

ISO 9001:2015 Reference	Comments
9.3.2	These are the details of the subject of the management review. There are several additional requirements.
Management review inputs	
	Italicized text denotes no change in requirements.

Requirement	How defined/documented and controlled?	Need to implement	Needs work/ revision	OK
Management review shall be planned.				
Take into consideration:				
• *Status of actions from previous reviews*				
• Changes in external and internal issues that are relevant to the QMS				
• Customer satisfaction and feedback from relevant interested parties				
• Extent to which quality objectives have been met				
• *Nonconformities and corrective actions*				
• Monitoring and measurement results				
• *Audit results*				
• Performance of suppliers				
• Adequacy of resources				
• Effectiveness of actions taken to address risks and opportunities				
• Opportunities for improvement				

Notes

Notes

GAP ANALYSIS WORK SHEET 9.3.3

ISO 9001:2015 Reference	Comments
9.3.3 Management review outputs	There have been only small changes in the requirements for management review outputs. *Italicized text denotes no change in requirements.*

Requirement	How defined/documented and controlled?	Need to implement	Needs work/ revision	OK
Outputs shall include: • Opportunities for improvement				
• Need to change the QMS				
• *Resource needs*				

Notes

Notes

GAP ANALYSIS WORK SHEET 10.1

ISO 9001:2015 Reference	Comments
10.1	The language relating to improvement has changed with the addition of more prescriptive requirements.
Improvement—General	

Requirement	How defined/documented and controlled?	Need to implement	Needs work/ revision	OK
Determine and select opportunities for improvement.				
Implement any necessary actions to meet customer requirements and enhance customer satisfaction, including: • Improving products and services to meet requirements and address future needs and expectations				
• Correcting, preventing, or reducing undesired effects				
• Improving the performance and effectiveness of the QMS				

Notes

Notes

GAP ANALYSIS WORK SHEET 10.2.1

ISO 9001:2015 Reference	Comments
10.2.1 Nonconformity and corrective action	This subclause contains much of the corrective action requirements from ISO 9001:2008 with additional requirements. *Italicized text denotes no change in requirements.*

Requirement	How defined/documented and controlled?	Need to implement	Needs work/ revision	OK
When a nonconformity occurs, react by: • Taking action to control and correct				
• Dealing with consequences				
Evaluate need for action to eliminate cause(s) of nonconformity, so it doesn't recur or occur elsewhere. • Review and analyze nonconformity.				
• *Determine causes.*				
• Determine if similar nonconformities exist or could potentially occur.				
Implement any action needed.				
Review the effectiveness of any corrective action taken.				
Update risks and opportunities determined during planning.				
Make changes to QMS, if necessary.				
Ensure actions appropriate to effects of nonconformities.				

Notes

Notes

GAP ANALYSIS WORK SHEET 10.2.2

ISO 9001:2015 Reference	Comments
10.2.2	These requirements relate to retention of documented information.
Nonconformity and corrective action	*Italicized text denotes no change in requirements.*

Requirement	How defined/documented and controlled?	Need to implement	Needs work/ revision	OK
Retain documented information relating to: • *Nature of nonconformity and any subsequent action*				
• *Results of corrective action*				

Notes

Notes

GAP ANALYSIS WORK SHEET 10.3

ISO 9001:2015 Reference	Comments
10.3 Continual improvement	The requirements relating to continual improvement are mostly unchanged except for the addition of language about needs and opportunities. *Italicized text denotes no change in requirements.*

Requirement	How defined/documented and controlled?	Need to implement	Needs work/ revision	OK
Continually improve the QMS.				
Consider results from analysis and evaluation, and management review.				
Address needs or opportunities.				

Notes

Chapter 6

Conclusion

The transition of your quality management system (QMS) from ISO 9001:2008 to ISO 9001:2015 should be perceived as a great opportunity to revitalize your system. The project can be rewarding and energizing.

The changes in this standard are better aligned with day-to-day business practices. The new requirements found in section 4 should bring more uniformity and control to processes that can bring value to your organization. Other changes ensure that your QMS will be more reflective of 21st century technology and global realities.

As you prepare for the transition audit, bear in mind that you had a good system to begin with. The changes you're making will only improve your QMS. Once you've completed your transition activities, you may contact your certification body (registrar) confident in the knowledge that your system complies with the 2015 standard and that your assessment audit will validate the effectiveness and integrity of your QMS.

Good luck!

www.ingramcontent.com/pod-product-compliance
Lightning Source LLC
Chambersburg PA
CBHW080241270326

41926CB00020B/4326